Lions are the king of beasts. These magnificent big cats once roamed Africa, Asia, and Europe. Now they only live in central and southern Africa and the Gir Forest National Park in India. There is only one species of lion.

Discover **10** reasons to love them!

female lion (lioness)

male lion

① They hang out together

Unlike all other cats, lions live and hunt together in family groups called prides. All the lionesses and their young are related, and they hang out with up to three different males.

lioness

lion

acacia tree

In Africa, each pride patrols huge territories of sunbaked savanna.

cubs

2 They have magnificent manes

Male lions must fight each other to be the leader of the pride. They have shaggy manes that protect them from fierce bites and scratches. Two males can rule together, but sometimes just one lion will be in charge.

young male

mane

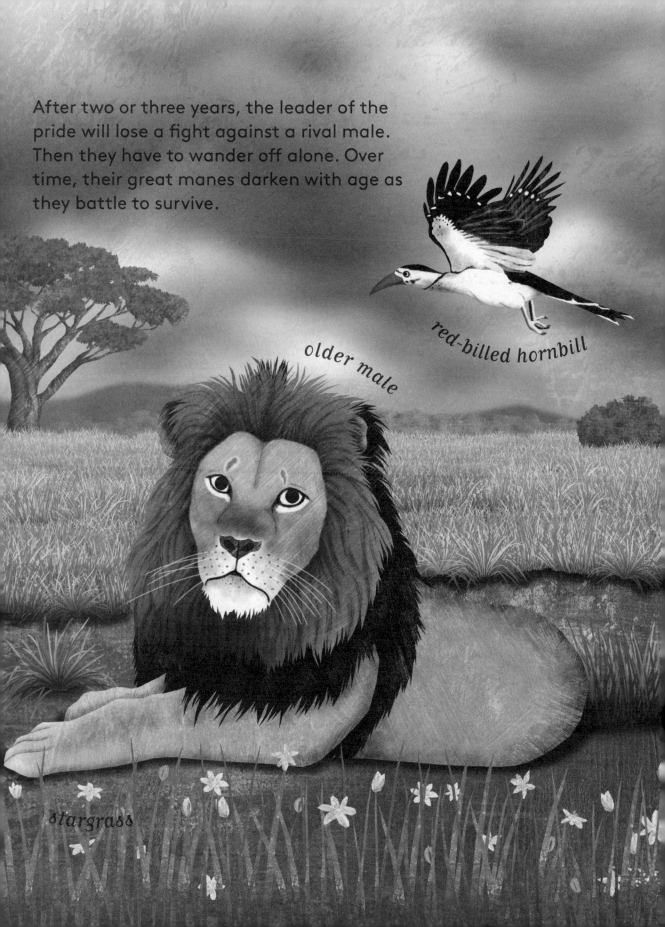

After two or three years, the leader of the pride will lose a fight against a rival male. Then they have to wander off alone. Over time, their great manes darken with age as they battle to survive.

red-billed hornbill

older male

stargrass

3 They have a mighty roar

As day breaks or dusk falls, male lions stretch back and roar. They are warning rivals or calling out to their pride. This mighty sound can raise a cloud of dust and be heard five miles away.

tassel

flycatcher bird

SHOW YOU LOVE A LION

Ask for a lion for your birthday! Adopt a lion through charity organizations to get fact packs and updates.

Lions also send messages with their tails. They flick them if they are mad and raise their black tassels so cubs can follow them through the long grass.

tail

4 They think spikes are scary

Lions like eating porcupines, but these prickly meals are difficult to catch. They try to flip the porcupines over with their paws. But in this dance to survive, the porcupine quills often get stuck in the lion's paws, nose, or cheek.

porcupine

indian cobra

If these barbed spikes sink deep into a lion's skin, they can lead to deadly infections. If the porcupine escapes, it simply grows more quills. So apart from humans, porcupines are a lion's worst enemy.

teak tree

lioness

5 They have glow-in-the-dark eyes

A few days after they are born, lion cubs open their blue-gray eyes. Months later, these turn orangey brown and shine in the dark. Lions are nocturnal and need to be able to see in dim light.

lion

moon

lesser
bush baby

pangolin

Small patches of white fur reflect low light back into a
lion's eyes. This helps them see better so they can find
and track their prey in the cool shadows of the night.

hyena

vulture

zebra

SHOW YOU LOVE A LION

Send Lions
for Life cards!
Support the Born
Free Foundation
and help spread
the word.

6 The females are the hunters

When their cubs are hungry, lionesses slink off to hunt. They scan the landscape for the opportunity of a meal. As a team, these camouflaged cats can bring down zebras, antelope, or even a giraffe.

When they spot their prey, each lioness knows exactly what to do. Some race ahead to wait in ambush while others herd the victim into their clever trap. Their success will feed the pride.

lioness

7 They have playful cubs

Lion cubs tumble over their patient, resting mothers. They chase her tail and lick her face. They fight for fun or may play with an ostrich egg that they find in the grass.

gazelle

cubs

Bouncy cubs are healthy and strong. But all lion cubs are in danger if their father, the leader of the pride, loses a fight. A new male will only want his own cubs in his pride.

ostrich

ostrich egg

They love a catnap

Lions spend a lot of their time asleep. They cuddle up together, stretch out, or just flop in a pile. Some seek the shade, while others loll in the sun or hang over a branch up a tree.

If their tummies are full with a really big meal, lions slumber all day and all night...

lilac-breasted roller

cub

warthog

lioness

lion

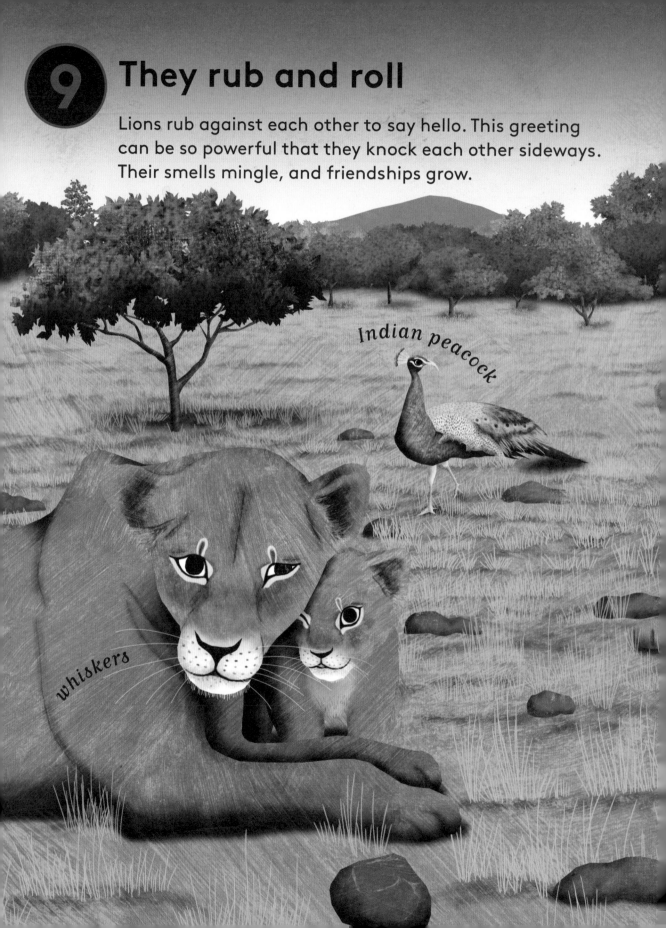

9 They rub and roll

Lions rub against each other to say hello. This greeting can be so powerful that they knock each other sideways. Their smells mingle, and friendships grow.

Indian peacock

whiskers

Each lion has its own oily scent. This special smell comes from its chin, lips, cheeks, whiskers, tail, and even the area between its toes.

SHOW YOU LOVE A LION

Buy recycled lion poop pellets! They are said to frighten stray cats away, as they think a bigger cat is on the prowl.

mugger crocodile

lions

10 They rule their land

Lions are top predators in the wild places where they live. But the survival of these big cats is threatened by trophy hunters and farms expanding into the natural habitats where lions roam.

zebra

lion